Published by Creative Education
P.O. Box 227, Mankato, Minnesota 56002
Creative Education is an imprint of
The Creative Company
www.thecreativecompany.us

Design by The Design Lab
Production by Chelsey Luther
Art direction by Rita Marshall
Printed in the United States of America

Photographs by Animals Animals (John Lemker),
Dreamstime (Odelia Cohen, Henri Faure, Jeremy
Richards, Samrat35, Johannes Gerhardus Swanepoel,
Willi1972), Getty Images (Mattias Klum, Nicholas
Parfitt, Joel Sartore, ZSSD), iStockphoto (Peter
Malsbury, Pauline S Mills), Shutterstock (Johan
Swanepoel)

Library of Congress Cataloging-in-Publication Data
Bodden, Valerie.
Rhinoceroses / by Valerie Bodden.
p. cm. — (Amazing animals)
Summary: A basic exploration of the appearance,
behavior, and habitat of rhinoceroses, the famously
horned animals. Also included is a story from folklore
explaining why rhinos have bumpy skin.
Includes bibliographical references and index.
ISBN 978-1-60818-090-5
1. Rhinoceroses—Juvenile literature. I. Title.
QL737.U63B63 2013
599.66'8—dc23   2011050276

CPSIA: 040913 PO1675

9 8 7 6 5 4 3 2

AMAZING ANIMALS

RHINOCEROSES

BY VALERIE BODDEN

CREATIVE EDUCATION

Elephants live in some of the same parts of Africa as rhinos

Rhinoceroses are the second-biggest land **mammals** in the world. Only elephants are bigger. There are five kinds of rhinoceros in the world. People call them "rhinos" for short.

mammals animals that have hair or fur and feed their babies with milk

All rhinos have one or two horns on their nose. Rhinos have thick, gray or brown skin and short legs. They have small eyes and cannot see very well.

The word "rhinoceros"
means "nose horn"

Rhinos can be from 4.5 to 6.5 feet (1.4–2 m) tall. They can weigh 1,700 to 7,000 pounds (771–3,175 kg). Even though they are so big, rhinos can run 28 miles (45 km) per hour or even faster! But they do not run far.

Black rhinos can run almost 40 miles (64 km) per hour

*The two kinds of African
rhinos have two horns*

Rhinos live on the **continents** of Africa and Asia. Most live in flat, hot grasslands called savannas. Others live in forests or **rainforests**. Some rhinos live at the base of **mountains**.

continents Earth's seven big pieces of land

mountains very big hills made of rock

rainforests forests with many trees and lots of rain

All rhinos eat plants. Some eat short grasses. Others feed on small bushes and trees. Rhinos can eat 90 pounds (41 kg) of food a day!

Rhinoceros teeth are good for chewing leafy foods

Female rhinos have one baby, called a calf, at a time. The calf weighs 55 to 100 pounds (25–45 kg) when it is born! Mother rhinos guard their calves from lions, tigers, hyenas, and crocodiles. Calves stay with their mothers for three to five years. Wild rhinos can live 25 to 40 years.

A rhino calf can stand an hour after it is born

Most rhinos live alone. Rhinos commonly feed in the early morning and in the evening. Rhinos that live in Africa sometimes have to walk for days to find water to drink.

A rhino finds water at a watering hole or river

Oxpeckers help rhinos and other large animals get rid of pests

Rhinos like to wallow, or roll, in pools of mud. The mud cools their skin. It also keeps them safe from biting flies. Birds called oxpeckers eat **parasites** off a rhino's back.

parasites animals that live on or in other animals and take food from them

There are not many rhinos left in the world. Many have been killed for their horns. But today some people go to see wild rhinos. They have to be careful not to get too close. Otherwise the rhinos might charge! Other people visit rhinos at zoos. It can be fun to watch these big animals eat, sleep, and wallow!

Male rhinos sometimes fight each other over females

A Rhinoceros Story

Why does the rhinoceros have bumpy, folded skin? People in Africa used to tell a story about this. They said that long ago, an elephant and a rhino got in a fight. The rhino's skin got many cuts. He used a porcupine needle to sew up his skin. When he was done, the rhino had big, uneven scars on his side. And since then, all rhinoceroses have had bumpy skin!

Read More

Galvin, Laura Gates. *Alphabet of African Animals*. Norwalk, Conn.: Soundprints, 2010.

Hamilton, Garry. *Rhino Rescue*. Buffalo, N.Y.: Firefly Books, 2006.

Pipe, Jim. *Conservation: Animals in Danger*. North Mankato, Minn.: Stargazer Books, 2008.

Web Sites

National Geographic Kids Creature Features: Black Rhinoceroses
http://kids.nationalgeographic.com/kids/animals/creaturefeature/black-rhinoceros/
This site has facts, pictures, and videos of black rhinos.

San Diego Zoo Kids: Rhinoceros
http://kids.sandiegozoo.org/animals/mammals/rhinoceros
This site has rhino pictures and information.

Index